GERARD MANLEY HOPKINS

Look up at the Skies!

Poems and prose chosen and introduced by

Rex Warner

ILL
Yv

D1439175

THE BODLEY HEAD
LONDON SYDNEY
TORONTO

This selection and introduction © Rex Warner 1972
Illustrations © The Bodley Head Ltd 1972
ISBN 0 370 01259 3
Printed and bound in Great Britain for
The Bodley Head Ltd
9 Bow Street, London WC2E7AL
by W & J Mackay Limited, Chatham
Set in 'Monotype' Baskerville
This selection first published 1972

LOOK UP AT THE SKIES!

First Published Nov. 1972

Introduction by

REX WARNER

Many great poets have come into their full fame after their death, but most of these have enjoyed at least some kind of recognition from the public during their lifetimes. Gerard Manley Hopkins in his short life (1844–1889) was entirely unknown as a poet, except to two or three friends. Some twenty years after his death one of these friends, the Poet Laureate Robert Bridges, edited a volume of poems written by Hopkins in the years 1876–1889, and since the date of their publication in 1918, their fame and influence has spread with extraordinary rapidity. No reader or writer of poetry in English today can fail to have felt the influence of this great Victorian poet whom the great Victorians had never heard of and whom even his best friends found often too difficult to read.

Today, owing to greater familiarity and perhaps also to the fact that some of his idiosyncrasies (though scarcely ever his genuine touch) have been so often imitated, most people do not find him difficult. But those who first came across his poems in the twenties will recall the shock of delighted surprise with which they recognised, or seemed to recognise, something wildly exciting and almost utterly new.

Youth is, fortunately, apt to resent what it conceives to be injustice and is as anxious to find persecutors and enemies as friends and benefactors. But it is not always accurate in its search for scapegoats. As a young man, I, for instance, would blame Bridges for not having brought out the poems earlier, the Jesuits, of whose Society Hopkins was one, for not having given greater encouragement to him, the editors of the Catholic review *The Month* for having rejected the only two poems he ever submitted for publication, and, indeed, the whole

Victorian 'establishment'. This hasty attribution of guilt was, to say the least, utterly unfair. Bridges was a devoted friend and a careful editor; without him the poetry might well have been lost for ever. There is no evidence of oppression, but much of kindness and encouragement in the treatment given to the poet by the Jesuits. And an editor can scarcely be blamed for not publishing work which was not only unintelligible to him, but which he had reason to believe would be equally unintelligible to his readers. As for the Victorian 'establishment', Hopkins and many of his friends looked upon it in many aspects with horror or distaste. But his feelings were not quite revolutionary. The England to which he was devoted was the England whose particular beauty and character were derived from a Christian tradition and from the idea of a 'gentleman'. Like so many great artists, he is able to combine qualities which are often thought of as contradictory. He can be looked at as a conservative and also as a revolutionary, as belonging both to the future and to the past. What has been considered as 'obscurity' in his poetry is often seen to arise from the simplest, freshest and purest expression of his vision. And when he appears to be writing, as he sometimes, though not often, does, in a loose, 'natural' and unconventional way, he is in fact weighing every word and every stress. What looked at first sight haphazard is finely and carefully wrought.

Bridges, for example, when he first read the poem called 'The Leaden Echo and the Golden Echo' (see p. 36) was reminded by what seemed to him its loose versification of the poetry of Walt Whitman and asked Hopkins whether he had been influenced by that poet. The first lines of Hopkins' poem read:

How to kéep—is there ány any, is there none such, nowhere
    known some, bow or brooch or braid or brace, láce, latch
    or catch or key to keep
Back beauty, keep it, beauty, beauty, beauty, . . . from
    vanishing away?
Ó is there no frowning of these wrinkles, rankèd wrinkles deep,

Dówn? no waving off of these most mournful messengers, still
messengers, sad and stealing messengers of grey?

Odd as it is that anyone should mistake these lines, with
their marked rhythm and rhyme, for 'free verse', Bridges did
stumble on a strange affinity between Hopkins and Whitman,
though it was not the affinity that he imagined. In a letter
replying to his friend, Hopkins, after saying that he cannot
have read more than half a dozen poems of Whitman, rather
surprisingly, and amusingly, adds: 'But first I may as well say
what I should not otherwise have said, that I always knew in
my heart Walt Whitman's mind to be more like my own than
any other man's living. As he is a very great scoundrel this is
not a pleasant confession. And this also makes me the more
desirous to read him and the more determined that I will not.'

Later in the same letter he claims that, while his own art is
conscious and elaborate, that of Whitman, whatever its
merits, is 'savage'. He goes on to say: 'Extremes meet, and
(I must for truth's sake say what sounds pride) this savagery
of his art, this rhythm in its last ruggedness and decomposi-
tion into common prose, comes near the last elaboration of
mine. For that piece of mine is very highly wrought. The
long lines are not rhythm run to seed: everything is weighed
and timed in them. Wait till they have taken hold of your ear
and you will find it so.'

This advice, to 'wait till the lines have taken hold of your
ear', is the best advice that can be given to readers of Hopkins. It is constantly repeated. In another letter to Bridges
(August 1877) he writes: 'My verse is less to be read than
heard, as I have told you before.' And he is perfectly confi-
dent that, if his advice is taken, most imagined difficulties will
disappear. Bridges apparently has suggested some alterations
and the reply is: 'I cannot think of altering anything. Why
shd. I? I do not write for the public. You are my public and
I hope to convert you.' In the end, and very fortunately, he
did succeed in converting Bridges, but it is likely that this
conversion would have taken place earlier if Bridges had

7

earlier been able to take his friend's advice. For once the lines have 'taken hold of' one's ear, one will find that the meaning also will often become easy where at first it may have seemed difficult. And the difficulties of rhythm will always disappear.

Much has been written about the 'sprung rhythm' which Hopkins claims, if not to have invented, to have brought back again into English poetry after a long lapse of time. (See his letter to R. W. Dixon, p. 59.) This rhythm, which he regards as the most 'natural', he finds in a number of times and places, in the ancient Greek lyrics of Pindar and the tragic writers, in Anglo-Saxon poetry, in nursery rhymes, in Welsh prosody and, most particularly and consciously employed, in Milton, especially in the choruses of 'Samson Agonistes'. Hopkins and Milton are alike in being both great scholars and great technicians. The differences between them on politics and on religion are, of course, enormous, but Hopkins' admiration for the older poet seems to have been so great that he never, as in the case of Whitman, refers to Milton as 'a very great scoundrel', heretic and regicide as he may be.

As in Milton, and in Shakespeare too, there are passages in Hopkins which are not easy fully to understand. Sometimes this may be because of an unusual order of words, where one word is singled out for particular emphasis either by stress or by position (as is a common practice in Greek and Latin poetry); sometimes the syntax is, or seems to be, strange or impossible (though Hopkins could always defend it); and sometimes the difficulty will come simply from the intensity of the thought or the immediacy of the vision. These difficulties will not prove discouraging if one follows Hopkins' advice of letting the lines 'take hold of' the ear. As he writes to Bridges (in a letter from which a longer extract is quoted on p. 57): 'Why, sometimes one enjoys and admires the very lines one cannot understand, as for instance "If it were done when 'tis done" sqq.,* which is all obscure and disputed, though how fine it is everybody sees and nobody disputes.' Exactly the
* *Macbeth*, I. vii. 1

8

same may be said of his own poem 'The Windhover' (see p. 25), the last six lines of which have been interpreted in at least five or six different ways.

More often what may at first seem a strangeness in language is soon recognised as only strange because it is unusually clear, forcible and sensitive. For instance that beautiful unfinished 'Epithalamion' (see p. 51), which was written in the year before his death, brims over with a delighted joy in the exercise of every sense and the style is appropriate to this ecstatic vision. The simple or ordinary action of a man who, on a hot summer's day, finds a pool in the bed of a stream among the woods and decides to undress and enjoy a bathe is dignified and made splendid and almost sacramental by language which may at times remind one of obscure locutions of Aeschylus, but which is utterly clear and utterly Hopkins' own.

. . . Here he feasts: lovely all is! No more: off with—down
   he dings
His bleachèd both and woolwoven wear:
Careless these in coloured wisp
All lie tumbled-to; then with loop-locks
Forward falling, forehead frowning, lips crisp
Over finger-teasing task, his twiny boots
Fast he opens, last he off wrings
Till walk the world he can with bare his feet . . .

In the poetry of his printed in this book I have only included complete poems (except for some which, like the 'Epithalamion', were never completed). This has meant the exclusion of one important long poem, 'The Wreck of the Deutschland'. It was tempting to include at least some stanzas of this powerful piece, but, beautiful and thrilling as individual stanzas are, their full beauty and the full force of their religious inspiration can only be felt if the poem is read in its entirety.

In most poems, indeed in all of them, the reader will note

the poet's delighted appreciation of the essential inner and particular nature of things—a feeling or vision for which in his Journal he uses the words 'inscape' and 'instress'. The words are not always used entirely consistently, but they serve to indicate the feeling for what is unique, what makes a thing to be firmly and decisively 'this thing' and not any other thing or a mere example of a class of things. Yet all the brilliant distinction and variety are seen together as a hymn to God and for His greater glory.

> All things counter, original, spare, strange;
> Whatever is fickle, freckled (who knows how?)
> With swift, slow; sweet, sour; adazzle, dim;
> He fathers-forth whose beauty is past change:
> Praise him.

Hopkins is pre-eminently a religious poet and his religion gave meaning to his whole life. What it meant to him is more accessible to us through his poetry and prose than it can be by reading a biography which, in the nature of things, cannot reveal to us at this distance more than the bare outline of so rich a personality. But in order to see him in the context of his times, some biographical facts may be of interest.

He was born in 1844 at Stratford, Essex, the eldest of a family of eight children. His family was well-to-do and culti-vated. Two of the brothers became professional artists and Gerard Hopkins was not only a gifted draughtsman but also a musician. His schooldays at Highgate School appear to have been happy and distinguished. He won the Poetry Prize in 1860 and in 1863 went up to Balliol College Oxford with an Exhibition in Classics. He was a fine scholar and got a 'First' in both Honour Mods. and, in 1867, in 'Greats'. At Oxford he first made friends with Robert Bridges. Other important influences were Benjamin Jowett, the Master of Balliol, Regius Professor of Greek and one of the chief leaders of the 'liberal rationalists' in the Protestant church; Walter Pater, proponent of 'aestheticism', who was one of his tutors; and, in particular, Dr Pusey, the leader of the Anglo-Catholic movement which at the time had been weakened both by the departure of Newman to join the Church of Rome and, on the other side, by the growing influence of the 'liberal rationalism' of Jowett and his party. Some of Hopkins' own difficulties and his final decision are noted in the Journal which he kept from 1866 to 1875. It was in 1866 that he made his decision and was received into the Catholic Church by Newman. In 1868, after taking his degree and enjoying a holiday in Switzerland, he entered the Society of Jesus and began his nine years' training for the priesthood. At this stage of his life he burnt (or thought that he had burnt) all his early poems (as recorded in the letter to R. W. Dixon quoted on p. 59). In fact some of these have survived and provide sure evidence of his great ability as a poet. Yet his full power seems to have developed in silence. For seven years he wrote nothing and then, at the instigation of his superiors in the Society of Jesus, composed 'The Wreck of the Deutschland'. In this poem we see for the first time Hopkins' mature style; but even Bridges could make little of it either then or for years afterwards (see Hopkins' letter to him on p. 57). During his training in medieval philosophy he became acquainted with the work of Duns Scotus and found in him a brother-soul whose doctrine of the 'thisness' of individual things corresponded with and threw light on his own thought and feeling.

In 1877 he was ordained priest and for some five years worked in parishes in London, Oxford, the north of England and Scotland. His health was never robust and he found the work hard. He was dispirited by the conditions in which the workers in the industrial towns lived, though he often found their lives, particularly in the northern cities, warmer and richer than those of his more 'respectable' parishioners in easier circumstances. In 1882 he was appointed to teach Classics at Stonyhurst College in Lancashire and two years later became Professor of Classics at University College, Dublin. His health did not improve and, as some of his letters show, he felt himself peculiarly isolated in Ireland, disapproving both of the anti-English sentiment of many of the Catholic clergy and also of the efforts of Gladstone (the 'traitor') to improve matters by granting Home Rule, although he felt keenly the injustices which the Irish had experienced from the English. If one may judge from the sonnets of 1885 (see pp. 39–44), he also seems to have experienced at this time some kind of crisis of faith (as have many of the great mystics) and a general despair both of the world and of his own action in it. Yet this was certainly not his dominant mood in his last years. Nothing he wrote is more full of life and joy than the 'Epithalamion' of 1888. Early in the next year he became seriously ill and his condition worsened until in June he died, declaring in his last words 'I am so happy, so happy'.

REX WARNER

Acknowledgments

The poems in this selection are reprinted from the *Poems of Gerard Manley Hopkins* (4th edition) edited by W. H. Gardner and N. H. MacKenzie, the Journal extracts from *The Journals and Papers of Gerard Manley Hopkins* edited by Humphry House, completed by Graham Storey, and the letters from *The Letters of Gerard Manley Hopkins to Robert Bridges*, and the *Correspondence of Gerard Manley Hopkins and Richard Watson Dixon* both edited by Claude Colleer Abbott, all published by Oxford University Press by arrangement with the Society of Jesus.

Contents

FROM THE LETTERS

FROM THE *JOURNAL*

Hopkins' Journal was kept from May 1866 to February 1875. For most of this time he had given up the writing of poetry, but the Journal is full of his close and particular observation of nature (in which he resembles many of the Victorians and, especially, Ruskin). Here too we find his first reference to what he calls 'inscape', a word which clarifies to him the essence and the feeling of his vision. Many of the impressions which he notes were to be incorporated in his later poems.

In May 1866 Hopkins was still an undergraduate at Balliol College, Oxford. This first extract was written later in that year.

July 1. Sharp showers, bright between. Late in the afternoon the light and shade being brilliant, snowy blocks of cloud were filing over the sky, and under the sun hanging above and along the earth-line were those multitudinous up-and-down crispy sparkling chains with pearly shadows up to the edges. At sunset, which was in a grey bank with moist gold dabs and racks, the whole round of skyline had level clouds naturally lead-colour but the upper parts ruddled, some more, some less, rosy. Spits or beams braided or built in with slanting pellet flakes made their way. Through such clouds anvil-shaped pink ones and up-blown fleece-of-wool flat-topped dangerous-looking pieces.

A year later, in 1867, having taken his degree and left Oxford, he was on holiday in Devon.

Aug. 30. Fair; in afternoon fine; the clouds had a good deal of crisping and mottling. – A round by Plumley.* – Stands of ash in a copse: they consisted of two or three rods most gracefully leaved, for each wing or comb finally curled inwards,

* A village in Devonshire

that is upwards. – Putting my hand up against the sky whilst we lay on the grass I saw more richness and beauty in the blue than I had known of before, not brilliance but glow and colour. It was not transparent and sapphire-like but turquoise-like, swarming and blushing round the edge of the hand and in the pieces clipped in by the fingers, the flesh being sometimes sunlit, sometimes glassy with reflected light, sometimes lightly shadowed in that violet one makes with cobalt and Indian red.

In 1868 with an Oxford friend he went to Switzerland for a holiday and described a walk up the valley of the Aar . . .

July 19. At times the valley opened in *cirques*, amphitheatres, enclosing levels of plain, and the river then ran between flaky flat-fish isles made of cindery lily-white stones. – In or near one of these openings the guide cries out 'Voulez-vous une Alp-rose?' and up he springs the side of the hill and brings us each bunches of flowers down.

In one place over a smooth table of rock came slipping down a blade of water looking like and as evenly crisped as fruitnets let drop and falling slack.

We saw Handeck waterfall. It is in fact the meeting of two waters, the right the Aar sallow and jade-coloured, the left a smaller stream of clear lilac foam. It is the greatest fall we have seen. The lower half is hidden in spray. I watched the great bushes of foam-water, the texture of branchings and water-spandrils which makes them up. At their outsides nearest the rock they gave off showers of drops strung together into little quills which sprang out in fans.

On crossing the Aar again there was as good a fall as some we have paid to see, all in jostling foam-bags.

Across the valley too we saw the fall of the Gelmer – like milk chasing round blocks of coal; or a girdle or long purse of white weighted with irregular black rubies, carelessly thrown aside and lying in jutty bends, with a black clasp of the same stone at the top – for those were the biggest blocks, squared, and built up, as it happened, in lessening stories, and the cascade enclosed them on the right and left hand with its foam; or once more like the skin of a white snake square-pied with black.

July 20. Fine.

Walked down to the Rhone glacier. It has three stages – first a smoothly-moulded bed in a pan or theatre of thorny peaks, swells of ice rising through the snow-sheet and the snow itself tossing and fretting into the sides of the rock walls in spray-like points: this is the first stage of the glaciers generally; it is like bright-plucked water swaying in a pail – ; second, after a slope nearly covered with landslips of moraine, was a ruck of horned waves steep and narrow in the gut: now in the upper Grindelwald glacier between the bed or highest stage was a descending limb which was like the rude and knotty bossings of a strombus shell – ; third the foot, a broad limb opening out and reaching the plain, shaped like the fan-fin of a dolphin or a great bivalve shell turned on its face, the flutings in either case being suggested by the crevasses and the ribs by the risings between them, these being swerved and inscaped strictly to the motion of the mass. Or you may compare the three stages to the heel, instep, and ball or toes of a foot. – The second stage looked at from nearer appeared like a box of plaster of Paris or starch or toothpowder, a little moist, tilted up and then struck and jarred so that the powder broke and tumbled in shapes and rifts.

We went into the grotto and also the vault from which the Rhone flows. It looked like a blue tent and as you went further in changed to lilac. As you come out the daylight glazes the groins with gleaming rosecolour. The ice inside has a branchy wire texture. The man shewed us the odd way in which a little piece of ice will stick against the walls – as if drawn by a magnet.

Standing on the glacier saw the prismatic colours in the clouds, and worth saying what sort of clouds: it was fine shapeless skins of fretted make, full of eyebrows or like linings of curled leaves which one finds in shelved corners of a wood.

17

After the holiday in Switzerland he entered the Novitiate of the Society of Jesus. Early in 1870 he was studying at Manresa House, Roehampton, Surrey, where he wrote the following entry:

Feb. One day in the Long Retreat (which ended on Xmas Day) they were reading in the refectory Sister Emmerich's account of the Agony in the Garden and I suddenly began to cry and sob and could not stop. I put it down for this reason, that if I had been asked a minute beforehand I should have said that nothing of the sort was going to happen and even when it did I stood in a manner wondering at myself not seeing in my reason the traces of an adequate cause for such strong emotion—the traces of it I say because of course the cause in itself is adequate for the sorrow of a lifetime. I remember much the same thing on Maundy Thursday when the presanctified Host was carried to the sacristy. But neither the weight nor the stress of sorrow, that is to say of the thing which should cause sorrow, by themselves move us or bring the tears as a sharp knife does not cut for being pressed as long as it is pressed without any shaking of the hand but there is always one touch, something striking sideways and unlooked for, which in both cases undoes resistance and pierces, and this may be so delicate that the pathos seems to have gone directly to the body and cleared the understanding in its passage. On the other hand the pathetic touch by itself, as in dramatic pathos, will only draw slight tears if its matter is not important or not of import to us, the strong emotion coming from a force which was gathered before it was discharged: in this way a knife may pierce the flesh which it had happened only to graze and only grazing will go no deeper.

From Manresa House it was not far to Richmond Park, to which Hopkins refers here:

May 18. Great brilliancy and projection: the eye seemed to fall perpendicular from level to level along our trees, the

18

nearer and further Park; all things hitting the sense with double but direct instress . . .

This was later. One day when the bluebells were in bloom I wrote the following. I do not think I have ever seen anything more beautiful than the bluebell I have been looking at. I know the beauty of our Lord by it. It[s inscape]* is [mixed of] strength and grace, like an ash [tree]. The head is strongly drawn over [backwards] and arched down like a cutwater [drawing itself back from the line of the keel]. The lines of the bells strike and overlie this, rayed but not symmetrically, some lie parallel. They look steely against [the] paper, the shades lying between the bells and behind the cockled petal-ends and nursing up the precision of their distinctness, the petal-ends themselves being delicately lit. Then there is the straightness of the trumpets in the bells softened by the slight entasis and [by] the square splay of the mouth. One bell, the lowest, some way detached and carried on a longer footstalk, touched out with the tips of the petals an oval/ not like the rest in a plane perpendicular to the axis of the bell but a little atilt, and so with [the] square-in-rounding turns of the petals. . . .
There is a little drawing of this detached bell. It looks square-cut in the original

In September 1870, having taken his first vows, he left Manresa House and went to the Roman Catholic seminary at Stonyhurst College in Lancashire. The next two entries were written at the College in the summer of the following year, 1871.

May 9 . . . This day and May 11 the bluebells in the little wood between the College and the highroad and in one of the Hurst Green cloughs. In the little wood/ opposite the light/ they stood in blackish spreads or sheddings like the spots on a snake. The heads are then like thongs and solemn in grain and grape-colour. But in the clough/ through the light/ they came in falls of sky-colour washing the brows and

* G. M. H.'s brackets

19

slacks of the ground with vein-blue, thickening at the double, vertical themselves and the young grass and brake fern combed vertical, but the brake struck the upright of all this with light winged transomes. It was a lovely sight. – The blue-bells in your hand baffle you with their inscape, made to every sense: if you draw your fingers through them they are lodged and struggle/ with a shock of wet heads; the long stalks rub and click and flatten to a fan on one another like your fingers themselves would when you passed the palms hard across one another, making a brittle rub and jostle like the noise of a hurdle strained by leaning against; then there is the faint honey smell and in the mouth the sweet gum when you bite them. But this is easy, it is the eye they baffle. They give one a fancy of pan-pipes and of some wind instrument with stops – a trombone perhaps. The overhung necks – for growing they are little more than a staff with a simple crook but in water, where they stiffen, they take stronger turns, in the head like sheephooks or, when more waved throughout, like the waves riding through a whip that is being smacked – what with these over-hung necks and what with the crisped ruffled bells dropping mostly on one side and the gloss these have at their footstalks they have an air of the knights at chess. Then the knot or 'knoop' of buds some shut, some just gaping, which makes the pencil of the whole spike, should be noticed: the inscape of the flower most finely carried out in the siding of the axes, each striking a greater and greater slant, is finished in these clus-tered buds, which for the most part are not straightened but rise to the end like a tongue and this and their tapering and a lit-tle flattening they have made them look like the heads of snakes

June (Later). The Horned Violet is a pretty thing, grace-fully lashed. Even in withering the flower ran through beautiful inscapes by the screwing up of the petals into straight little barrels or tubes. It is not that inscape does not govern the behaviour of things in slack and decay as one can see even in the pining of the skin in the old and even in a skeleton but that horror prepossesses the mind, but in this case there was nothing in itself to shew even whether the flower were shutting or opening

The 'pinion' of the blossom in the comfrey is remarkable for the beauty of the coil and its regular lessening to its centre. Perhaps the duller-coloured sorts shew it best

After examinations at the end of the summer term in 1872, Hopkins was on holiday on the Isle of Man where he made the next entry.

Aug. 10. I was looking at high waves. The breakers always are parallel to the coast and shape themselves to it except where the curve is sharp however the wind blows. They are rolled out by the shallowing shore just as a piece of putty between the palms whatever its shape runs into a long roll. The slant ruck or crease one sees in them shows the way of the wind. The regularity of the barrels surprised and charmed the eye; the edge behind the comb or crest was as smooth and bright as glass. It may be noticed to be green behind and silver white in front: the silver marks where the air begins, the pure white is foam, the green/ solid water. Then looked at to the right or left they are scrolled over like mouldboards or feathers or jibsails seen by the edge. It is pretty to see the hollow of the barrel disappearing as the white comb on each side runs along the wave gaining ground till the two meet at a pitch and crush and overlap each other

About all the turns of the scaping from the break and flooding of the wave to its run out again I have not yet satisfied myself. The shores are swimming and the eyes have before them a region of milky surf but it is hard for them to unpack the huddling and gnarls of the water and law out the shapes and the sequence of the running: I catch however the looped or forked wisp made by every big pebble the backwater runs over–if it were clear and smooth there would be a network from their overlapping, such as can in fact be seen on smooth sand after the tide is out–; then I saw it run browner, the foam dwindling and twitched into long chains of suds, while the strength of the backdraught shrugged the stones together and clocked them one against another

Looking from the cliff I saw well that work of dimpled foamlaps – strings of short loops or halfmoons – which I had studied at Freshwater years ago

It is pretty to see the dance and swagging of the light green tongues or ripples of waves in a place locked between rocks

The last two extracts included here were both written at Stony-hurst in the year 1873.

April 8. The ashtree growing in the corner of the garden was felled. It was lopped first: I heard the sound and looking out and seeing it maimed there came at that moment a great pang and I wished to die and not to see the inscapes of the world destroyed any more

June 16. I looked at the pigeons down in the kitchen yard and so on. They look like little gay jugs by shape when they walk, strutting and jod-jodding with their heads. The two young ones are all white and the pins of the folded wings, quill pleated over quill, are like crisp and shapely cuttleshells found on the shore. The others are dull thundercolour or black-grape-colour except in the white pieings, the quills and tail, and in the shot of the neck. I saw one up on the eaves of the roof: as it moved its head a crush of satin green came and went, a wet or soft flaming of the light

Sometimes I hear the cuckoo with wonderful clear and plump and fluty notes: it is when the hollow of a rising ground conceives them and palms them up and throws them out, like blowing into a big humming ewer – for instance under Saddle Hill one beautiful day and another time from Hodder wood when we walked on the other side of the river

THE POEMS

GOD'S GRANDEUR

THE world is charged with the grandeur of God.
  It will flame out, like shining from shook foil;
  It gathers to a greatness, like the ooze of oil
Crushed. Why do men then now not reck his rod?
Generations have trod, have trod, have trod;
  And all is seared with trade; bleared, smeared with toil;
  And wears man's smudge and shares man's smell: the soil
Is bare now, nor can foot feel, being shod.

And for all this, nature is never spent;
  There lives the dearest freshness deep down things;
And though the last lights off the black West went
  Oh, morning, at the brown brink eastward, springs—
Because the Holy Ghost over the bent
  World broods with warm breast and with ah! bright wings.

(*1877*)

THE STARLIGHT NIGHT

Look at the stars! look, look up at the skies!
    O look at all the fire-folk sitting in the air!
    The bright boroughs, the circle-citadels there!
Down in dim woods the diamond delves! the elves'-eyes!
The grey lawns cold where gold, where quickgold lies!
    Wind-beat whitebeam! airy abeles set on a flare!
    Flake-doves sent floating forth at a farmyard scare! –
Ah well! it is all a purchase, all is a prize.

Buy then! bid then! – What? – Prayer, patience, alms, vows.
Look, look: a May-mess, like on orchard boughs!
    Look! March-bloom, like on mealed-with-yellow sallows!
These are indeed the barn; withindoors house
The shocks. This piece-bright paling shuts the spouse
    Christ home, Christ and his mother and all his hallows.

                                                    (*1877*)

THE WINDHOVER:

To Christ our Lord

I CAUGHT this morning morning's minion, king-
 dom of daylight's dauphin, dapple-dawn-drawn Falcon, in
  his riding
 Of the rolling level underneath him steady air, and striding
High there, how he rung upon the rein of a wimpling wing
In his ecstasy! then off, off forth on swing,
 As a skate's heel sweeps smooth on a bow-bend: the hurl and
  gliding
 Rebuffed the big wind. My heart in hiding
Stirred for a bird, – the achieve of, the mastery of the thing!

Brute beauty and valour and act, oh, air, pride, plume, here
 Buckle! AND the fire that breaks from thee then, a billion
Times told lovelier, more dangerous, O my chevalier!

 No wonder of it: shéer plód makes plough down sillion
Shine, and blue-bleak embers, ah my dear,
 Fall, gall themselves, and gash gold-vermilion.

(May 30, 1877)

In his letters to Robert Bridges and to R. W. Dixon Hopkins often
used various marks and symbols to indicate how his poems should
be read (see p. 59). In this selection only a few of these marks, in-
dicating either stress or a break in the line, have been used.

PIED BEAUTY

GLORY be to God for dappled things –
  For skies of couple-colour as a brinded cow;
    For rose-moles all in stipple upon trout that swim;
Fresh-firecoal chestnut-falls; finches' wings;
  Landscape plotted and pieced – fold, fallow, and plough;
    And áll trádes, their gear and tackle and trim.
All things counter, original, spare, strange;
  Whatever is fickle, freckled (who knows how?)
    With swift, slow; sweet, sour; adazzle, dim;
He fathers-forth whose beauty is past change:
      Praise him.

(Summer, 1877)

HURRAHING IN HARVEST

SUMMER ends now; now, barbarous in beauty, the stooks rise
Around; up above, what wind-walks! what lovely behaviour
Of silk-sack clouds! has wilder, wilful-wavier
Meal-drift moulded ever and melted across skies?

I walk, I lift up, I lift up heart, eyes,
Down all that glory in the heavens to glean our Saviour;
And, éyes, heárt, what looks, what lips yet gave you a
Rapturous love's greeting of realer, of rounder replies?

And the azurous hung hills are his world-wielding shoulder
Majestic—as a stallion stalwart, very-violet-sweet!—
These things, these things were here and but the beholder
Wanting; which two when they once meet,
The heart rears wíngs bold and bolder
And hurls for him, O half hurls earth for him off under his feet.

(September 1, 1877)

BINSEY POPLARS

felled 1879

My aspens dear, whose airy cages quelled,
Quelled or quenched in leaves the leaping sun,
All felled, felled, are all felled;
    Of a fresh and following folded rank
        Not spared, not one
        That dandled a sandalled
      Shadow that swam or sank
On meadow and river and wind-wandering weed-
    winding bank.

  O if we but knew what we do
        When we delve or hew –
    Hack and rack the growing green!
        Since country is so tender
    To touch, her being só slender,
    That, like this sleek and seeing ball
    But a prick will make no eye at all,
    Where we, even where we mean
        To mend her we end her,
      When we hew or delve:
After-comers cannot guess the beauty been.
  Ten or twelve, only ten or twelve
    Strokes of havoc únselve
        The sweet especial scene,
    Rural scene, a rural scene,
    Sweet especial rural scene.

                        (March 1879)

DUNS SCOTUS'S OXFORD

TOWERY city and branchy between towers;
Cuckoo-echoing, bell-swarmèd, lark-charmèd, rook-racked,
    river-rounded;
The dapple-eared lily below thee; that country and town did
Once encounter in, here coped and poisèd powers;

Thou hast a base and brickish skirt there, sours
That neighbour-nature thy grey beauty is grounded
Best in; graceless growth, thou hast confounded
Rural rural keeping—folk, flocks, and flowers.

Yet ah! this air I gather and I release
He lived on; these weeds and waters, these walls are what
He haunted who of all men most sways my spirits to peace;

Of realty the rarest-veinèd unraveller; a not
Rivalled insight, be rival Italy or Greece;
Who fired France for Mary without spot.

(March 1879)

HENRY PURCELL

The poet wishes well to the divine genius of Purcell and praises him that, whereas other musicians have given utterance to the moods of man's mind, he has, beyond that, uttered in notes the very make and species of man as created both in him and in all men generally.

HAVE fair fallen, O fair, fair have fallen, so dear
To me, so arch-especial a spirit as heaves in Henry Purcell,
An age is now since passed, since parted; with the reversal
Of the outward sentence low lays him, listed to a heresy, here.

Not mood in him nor meaning, proud fire or sacred fear,
Or love or pity or all that sweet notes not his might nursle:
It is the forgèd feature finds me; it is the rehearsal
Of own, of abrúpt sélf there so thrusts on, so throngs the ear.

Let him oh! with his air of angels then lift me, lay me! only I'll
Have an eye to the sakes of him, quaint moonmarks, to his
    pelted plumage under
Wings: so some great stormfowl, whenever he has walked his
    while

The thunder-purple seabeach plumèd purple-of-thunder,
If a wuthering of his palmy snow-pinions scatter a
    colossal smile
Off him, but meaning motion fans fresh our wits with
    wonder.

                              (*April 1879*)

THE BUGLER'S FIRST COMMUNION

A BUGLER boy from barrack (it is over the hill
There) – boy bugler, born, he tells me, of Irish
    Mother to an English sire (he
Shares their best gifts surely, fall how things will),

This very very day came down to us after a boon he on
My late being there begged of me, overflowing
    Boon in my bestowing,
Came, I say, this day to it – to a First Communion.

Here he knelt then ín regimental red.
Forth Christ from cupboard fetched, how fain I of feet
    To his youngster take his treat!
Low-latched in leaf-light housel his too huge godhead.

There! and your sweetest sendings, ah divine,
By it, heavens, befall him! as a heart Christ's darling,dauntless;
    Tongue true, vaunt- and tauntless;
Breathing bloom of a chastity in mansex fine.

Frowning and forefending angel-warder
Squander the hell-rook ranks sally to molest him;
    March, kind comrade, abreast him;
Dress his days to a dexterous and starlight order.

How it dóes my heart good, visiting at that bleak hill,
When limber liquid youth, that to all I teach
    Yields tender as a pushed peach,
Hies headstrong to its wellbeing of a self-wise self-will!

Then though I should tread tufts of consolation
Dáys áfter, só I in a sort deserve to
    And do serve God to serve to
Just such slips of soldiery Christ's royal ration.

Nothing élse is like it, no, not all so strains
Us: freshyouth fretted in a bloomfall all portending
That sweet's sweeter ending;
Realm both Christ is heir to and thére réigns.

O now well work that sealing sacred ointment!
O for now charms, arms, what bans off bad
And locks love ever in a lad!
Let mé though see no more of him, and not disappointment

Those sweet hopes quell whose least me quickenings lift,
In scarlet or somewhere of some day seeing
That brow and bead of being,
An our day's God's own Galahad. Though this child's drift

Seems by a divíne doom chánnelled, nor do I cry
Disaster there; but may he not rankle and roam
In backwheels though bound home? –
That left to the Lord of the Eucharist, I here lie by;

Recorded only, I have put my lips on pleas
Would brandle adamantine heaven with ride and jar, did
Prayer go disregarded:
Forward-like, but however, and like favourable heaven heard
these.

(July 27? 1879)

FELIX RANDAL

FELIX RANDAL the farrier, O is he dead then? my duty all
    ended,
Who have watched his mould of man, big-boned and hardy-
    handsome
Pining, pining, till time when reason rambled in it and some
Fatal four disorders, fleshed there, all contended?

Sickness broke him. Impatient, he cursed at first, but mended
Being anointed and all; though a heavenlier heart began some
Months earlier, since I had our sweet reprieve and ransom
Tendered to him. Ah well, God rest him all road ever he
    offended!

This seeing the sick endears them to us, us too it endears.
My tongue had taught thee comfort, touch had quenched thy
    tears,
Thy tears that touched my heart, child, Felix, poor Felix
    Randal;

How far from then forethought of, all thy more boisterous years,
When thou at the random grim forge, powerful amidst peers,
Didst fettle for the great grey drayhorse his bright and battering
    sandal!

                              (April 28 1880)

SPRING AND FALL:

to a young child

MÁRGARÉT, áre you gríeving
Over Goldengrove unleaving?
Leáves, líke the things of man, you
With your fresh thoughts care for, can you?
Áh! ás the heart grows older
It will come to such sights colder
By and by, nor spare a sigh
Though worlds of wanwood leafmeal lie;
And yet you *will* weep and know why.
Now no matter, child, the name:
Sórrow's spríngs áre the same.
Nor mouth had, no nor mind, expressed
What heart heard of, ghost guessed:
It ís the blight man was born for,
It is Margaret you mourn for.

(September 7 1880)

'AS KINGFISHERS CATCH FIRE,
DRAGONFLIES DRAW FLAME'

As kingfishers catch fire, dragonflies draw flame;
    As tumbled over rim in roundy wells
    Stones ring; like each tucked string tells, each hung bell's
Bow swung finds tongue to fling out broad its name;
Each mortal thing does one thing and the same:
    Deals out that being indoors each one dwells;
    Selves—goes itself; *myself* it speaks and spells,
Crying *Whát I dó is me: for that I came.*

Í say more: the just man justices;
    Keeps gráce: thát keeps all his goings graces;
Acts in God's eye what in God's eye he is—
    Chríst. For Christ plays in ten thousand places,
Lovely in limbs, and lovely in eyes not his
    To the Father through the features of men's faces.

THE LEADEN ECHO

AND THE GOLDEN ECHO

(Maidens' song from St Winefred's Well)

THE LEADEN ECHO

H o w to kéep – is there ány any, is there none such, nowhere
    known some, bow or brooch or braid or brace, láce, latch
    or catch or key to keep
Back beauty, keep it, beauty, beauty, beauty, . . . from vanishing
    away?
Ó is there no frowning of these wrinkles, rankèd wrinkles deep,
Dówn? no waving off of these most mournful messengers, still
    messengers, sad and stealing messengers of grey? –
No there's none, there's none, O no there's none,
Nor can you long be, what you now are, called fair,
Do what you may do, what, do what you may,
And wisdom is early to despair:
Be beginning; since, no, nothing can be done
To keep at bay
Age and age's evils, hoar hair,
Ruck and wrinkle, drooping, dying, death's worst, winding
    sheets, tombs and worms and tumbling to decay;
So be beginning, be beginning to despair.
O there's none; no no no there's none:
Be beginning to despair, to despair,
Despair, despair, despair, despair.

THE GOLDEN ECHO
      Spare!
There ís one, yes I have one (Hush there!),
Only not within seeing of the sun.
Not within the singeing of the strong sun,

Tall sun's tingeing, or treacherous the tainting of the earth's air,
Somewhere elsewhere there is ah well where! one,
One. Yes I cán tell such a key, I dó know such a place,
Where whatever's prizèd and passes of us, everything that's
    fresh and fast flying of us, seems to us sweet of us and
    swiftly away with, done away with, undone,
Úndone, done with, soon done with, and yet dearly and
    dangerously sweet
Of us, the wimpled-water-dimpled, not-by-morning-matchèd
    face,
The flower of beauty, fleece of beauty, too too apt to, ah! to fleet,
Never fleets móre, fastened with the tenderest truth
To its own best being and its loveliness of youth: it is an ever-
    lastingness of, O it is an all youth!
Come then, your ways and airs and looks, locks, maidengear,
    gallantry and gaiety and grace,
Winning ways, airs innocent, maiden manners, sweet looks,
    loose locks, long locks, lovelocks, gaygear, going gallant,
    girlgrace—
Resign them, sign them, seal them, send them, motion them
    with breath,
And with sighs soaring, soaring síghs, deliver
Them; beauty-in-the-ghost, deliver it, early now, long before
    death
Give beauty back, beauty, beauty, beauty, back to God,
    beauty's self and beauty's giver.
See; not a hair is, not an eyelash, not the least lash lost; every
    hair
Is, hair of the head, numbered.
Nay, what we had lighthanded left in surly the mere mould
Will have waked and have waxed and have walked with the
    wind what while we slept,
This side, that side hurling a heavyheaded hundredfold
What while we, while we slumbered.

O then, weary then whý should we tread? O why are we so
     haggard at the heart, so care-coiled, care-killed, so fagged,
     so fashed, so cogged, so cumbered,
When the thing we freely fórfeit is kept with fonder a care,
Fonder a care kept than we could have kept it, kept
Far with fonder a care (and we, we should have lost it) finer,
     fonder
A care kept. – Where kept? do but tell us where kept, where. –
Yonder. – What high as that! We follow, now we follow. –
     Yonder, yes yonder, yonder,
Yonder.

                               (*October 13 1882*)

TO WHAT SERVES MORTAL BEAUTY?

To what serves mortal beauty I –dangerous; does set danc-
ing blood–the O-seal-that-so I feature, flung prouder form
Than Purcell tune lets tread to? I See: it does this: keeps warm
Men's wits to the things that are; I what good means–where a
    glance
Master more may than gaze, I gaze out of countenance.
Those lovely lads once, wet-fresh I windfalls of war's storm,
How then should Gregory, a father, I have gleanèd else from
    swarm-
èd Rome? But God to a nation I dealt that day's dear chance.
To man, that needs would worship I block or barren stone,
Our law says: Love what are I love's worthiest, were all known;
World's loveliest–men's selves. Self I flashes off frame and face.
What do then? how meet beauty? I Merely meet it; own,
Home at heart, heaven's sweet gift; I then leave, let that alone.
Yea, wish that though, wish all, I God's better beauty, grace.

(August 23 1885)

39

(CARRION COMFORT)

Not, I'll not, carrion comfort, Despair, not feast on thee;
Not untwist—slack they may be—these last strands of man
In me ór, most weary, cry *I can no more*. I can;
Can something, hope, wish day come, not choose not to be.

But ah, but O thou terrible, why wouldst thou rude on me
Thy wring-world right foot rock? lay a lionlimb against me? scan
With darksome devouring eyes my bruisèd bones? and fan,
O in turns of tempest, me heaped there; me frantic to avoid thee
    and flee?

Why? That my chaff might fly; my grain lie, sheer and clear.
Nay in all that toil, that coil, since (seems) I kissed the rod,
Hand rather, my heart lo! lapped strength, stole joy, would
    laugh, chéer.
Cheer whom though? The hero whose heaven-handling flung
    me, fóot tród
Me? or me that fought him? O which one? is it each one? That
    night, that year
Of now done darkness I wretch lay wrestling with (my God!)
    my God.

                                                    (?*1885*)

40

'NO WORST, THERE IS NONE,
PITCHED PAST PITCH OF GRIEF'

No worst, there is none. Pitched past pitch of grief,
More pangs will, schooled at forepangs, wilder wring.
Comforter, where, where is your comforting?
Mary, mother of us, where is your relief?
My cries heave, herds-long; huddle in a main, a chief-
woe, wórld-sorrow; on an áge-old anvil wince and sing –
Then lull, then leave off. Fury had shrieked 'No linge-
ring! Let me be fell: force I must be brief'.
O the mind, mind has mountains; cliffs of fall
Frightful, sheer, no-man-fathomed. Hold them cheap
May who ne'er hung there. Nor does long our small
Durance deal with that steep or deep. Here! creep,
Wretch, under a comfort serves in a whirlwind: all
Life death does end and each day dies with sleep.

(?1885)

'TO SEEM THE STRANGER
LIES MY LOT, MY LIFE'

To seem the stranger lies my lot, my life
Among strangers. Father and mother dear,
Brothers and sisters are in Christ not near
And he my peace/my parting, sword and strife.

England, whose honour O all my heart woos, wife
To my creating thought, would neither hear
Me, were I pleading, plead nor do I: I wear-
y of idle a being but by where wars are rife.

I am in Ireland now; now I am at a thírd
Remove. Not but in all removes I can
Kind love both give and get. Only what word

Wisest my heart breeds dark heaven's baffling ban
Bars or hell's spell thwarts. This to hoard unheard,
Heard unheeded, leaves me a lonely began.

(*?1885*)

'I WAKE
AND FEEL THE FELL OF DARK,
NOT DAY'

I WAKE and feel the fell of dark, not day.
What hours, O what black hoürs we have spent
This night! what sights you, heart, saw; ways you went!
And more must, in yet longer light's delay.

With witness I speak this. But where I say
Hours I mean years, mean life. And my lament
Is cries countless, cries like dead letters sent
To dearest him that lives alas! away.

I am gall, I am heartburn. God's most deep decree
Bitter would have me taste: my taste was me;
Bones built in me, flesh filled, blood brimmed the curse.

Selfyeast of spirit a dull dough sours. I see
The lost are like this, and their scourge to be
As I am mine, their sweating selves; but worse.

(?1885)

'MY OWN HEART
LET ME MORE HAVE PITY ON'

MY own heart let me more have pity on; let
Me live to my sad self hereafter kind,
Charitable; not live this tormented mind
With this tormented mind tormenting yet.

I cast for comfort I can no more get
By groping round my comfortless, than blind
Eyes in their dark can day or thirst can find
Thirst's all-in-all in all a world of wet.

Soul, self; come, poor Jackself, I do advise
You, jaded, let be; call off thoughts awhile
Elsewhere; leave comfort root-room; let joy size

At God knows when to God knows what; whose smile
's not wrung, see you; unforeseen times rather – as skies
Betweenpie mountains – lights a lovely mile.

(*?1885*)

THAT NATURE IS A HERACLITEAN FIRE
AND OF THE
COMFORT OF THE RESURRECTION

CLOUD-PUFFBALL, torn tufts, tossed pillows ∣ flaunt forth,
    then chevy on an air-
built thoroughfare: heaven-roysterers, in gay-gangs ∣ they
    throng; they glitter in marches.
Down roughcast, down dazzling whitewash, ∣ wherever an
    elm arches,
Shivelights and shadowtackle in long ∣ lashes lace, lance, and
    pair.
Delightfully the bright wind boisterous ∣ ropes, wrestles, beats
    earth bare
Of yestertempest's creases; ∣ in pool and rutpeel parches
Squandering ooze to squeezed ∣ dough, crust, dust; stanches,
    starches
Squadroned masks and manmarks ∣ treadmire toil there
Footfretted in it. Million-fuelèd, ∣ nature's bonfire burns on.
But quench her bonniest, dearest ∣ to her, her clearest-selvèd
    spark
Man, how fast his firedint, ∣ his mark on mind, is gone!
Both are in an unfathomable, all is in an enormous dark
Drowned. O pity and indig ∣ nation! Manshape, that shone
Sheer off, disseveral, a star, ∣ death blots black out; nor mark
               Is any of him at all so stark
But vastness blurs and time ∣ beats level. Enough! the
    Resurrection,
A heart's-clarion! Away grief's gasping, ∣ joyless days,
    dejection.
            Across my foundering deck shone
A beacon, an eternal beam. ∣ Flesh fade, and mortal trash
Fall to the residuary worm; ∣ world's wildfire, leave but ash:

In a flash, at a trumpet crash,
I am all at once what Christ is, ǀ since he was what I am, and
This Jack, joke, poor potsherd, ǀ patch, matchwood, immortal
diamond,
Is immortal diamond.

(*July 26 1888*)

In honour of

ST ALPHONSUS RODRIGUEZ

Laybrother of the Society of Jesus

HONOUR is flashed off exploit, so we say;
And those strokes once that gashed flesh or galled shield
Should tongue that time now, trumpet now that field,
And, on the fighter, forge his glorious day.
On Christ they do and on the martyr may;
But be the war within, the brand we wield
Unseen, the heroic breast not outward-steeled,
Earth hears no hurtle then from fiercest fray.
Yet God (that hews mountain and continent,
Earth, all, out; who, with trickling increment,
Veins violets and tall trees makes more and more)
Could crowd career with conquest while there went
Those years and years by of world without event
That in Majorca Alfonso watched the door.

(*1888*)

Justus quidem tu es, Domine, si disputem tecum; verumtamen
justa loquar ad te: Quare via impiorum prosperatur? &c.

THOU art indeed just, Lord, if I contend
With thee; but, sir, so what I plead is just.
Why do sinners' ways prosper? and why must
Disappointment all I endeavour end?

Wert thou my enemy, O thou my friend,
How wouldst thou worse, I wonder, than thou dost
Defeat, thwart me? Oh, the sots and thralls of lust
Do in spare hours more thrive than I that spend,

Sir, life upon thy cause. See, banks and brakes
Now, leavèd how thick! lacèd they are again
With fretty chervil, look, and fresh wind shakes

Them; birds build—but not I build; no, but strain,
Time's eunuch, and not breed one work that wakes.
Mine, O thou lord of life, send my roots rain.

                                        (*March 17 1889*)

THE WOODLARK

Teevo cheevo cheevio chee:
O where, what can thát be?
Weedio-weedio: there again!
So tiny a trickle of sóng-strain;
And all round not to be found
For brier, bough, furrow, or gréen ground
Before or behind or far or at hand
Either left either right
Anywhere in the súnlight.

Well, after all! Ah but hark—
'I am the little wóodlark.
The skylark is my cousin and he
Is known to men more than me.
Round a ring, around a ring
And while I sail (must listen) I sing.

To-day the sky is two and two
With white strokes and strains of the blue.
The blue wheat-acre is underneath
And the corn is corded and shoulders its sheaf,
The ear in milk, lush the sash,
And crush-silk poppies aflash,
The blood-gush blade-gash
Flame-rash rudred
Bud shelling or broad-shed
Tatter-tangled and dingle-a-danglèd
Dandy-hung dainty head.

And down ... the furrow dry
Sunspurge and oxeye
And lace-leaved lovely
Foam-tuft fumitory.

I ám so véry, O só very glád
That I dó thínk there is not to be had
[Anywhere any more joy to be in.
Cheevio :] when the cry within
Says Go on then I go on
Till the longing is less and the good gone,
But down drop, if it says Stop.
To the all-a-leaf of the tréetop.
And after that off the bough
[Hover-float to the hedge brow.]

Through the velvety wind V-winged
[Where shake shadow is sun's-eye-ringed]
To the nest's nook I balance and buoy
With a sweet joy of a sweet joy,
Sweet, of a sweet, of a sweet joy
Of a sweet – a sweet – sweet – joy.'

(*July 1876*)

EPITHALAMION

HARK, hearer, hear what I do; lend a thought now, make
    believe
We are leafwhelmed somewhere with the hood
Of some branchy bunchy bushybowered wood,
Southern dean or Lancashire clough or Devon cleave,
That leans along the loins of hills, where a candycoloured,
    where a gluegold-brown
Marbled river, boisterously beautiful, between
Roots and rocks is danced and dandled, all in froth and water-
    blowballs, down.
We are there, when we hear a shout
That the hanging honeysuck, the dogeared hazels in the cover
Makes dither, makes hover
And the riot of a rout
Of, it must be, boys from the town
Bathing: it is summer's sovereign good.

By there comes a listless stranger: beckoned by the noise
He drops towards the river: unseen
Sees the bevy of them, how the boys
With dare and with downdolphinry and bellbright bodies
    huddling out,
Are earthworld, airworld, waterworld thorough hurled, all
    by turn and turn about.

This garland of their gambol flashes in his breast
Into such a sudden zest
Of summertime joys
That he hies to a pool neighbouring; sees it is the best
There; sweetest, freshest, shadowiest;
Fairyland; silk-beech, scrolled ash, packed sycamore, wild
    wychelm, hornbeam fretty overstood

By. Rafts and rafts of flake leaves light, dealt so, painted on
  the air,
Hang as still as hawk or hawkmoth, as the stars or as the
  angels there,
Like the thing that never knew the earth, never off roots
Rose. Here he feasts: lovely all is! No more: off with–down
  he dings
His bleachèd both and woolwoven wear:
Careless these in coloured wisp
All lie tumbled-to; then with loop-locks
Forward falling, forehead frowning, lips crisp
Over finger-teasing task, his twiny boots
Fast he opens, last he off wrings
Till walk the world he can with bare his feet
And come where lies a coffer, burly all of blocks
Built of chancequarrièd, selfquainèd, hoar-huskèd rocks
And the water warbles over into, filleted | with glassy grassy
  quicksilvery shivès and shoots
And with heavenfallen freshness down from moorland still
  brims,
Dark or daylight on and on. Here he will then, here he will
  the fleet
Flinty kindcold element let break across his limbs
Long. Where we leave him, froliclavish, while he looks about
  him, laughs, swims.

Enough now; since the sacred matter that I mean
I should be wronging longer leaving it to float
Upon this only gambolling and echoing-of-earth note–

What is . . . the delightful dean?
Wedlock. What the water? Spousal love.

      .   .   .   .
      .   .   .   .

turns
Father, mother, brothers, sisters, friends
Into fairy trees, wildflowers, woodferns
Rankèd round the bower

. . . .

(1888)

FROM THE *LETTERS*

Hopkins' chief correspondent was, as one might expect, Robert Bridges, to whom he wrote with affection and freedom. The correspondence lasted from 1863 to 1889. Another important correspondent was R. W. Dixon, with whom Hopkins was barely acquainted when for a short time Dixon was a master at Highgate School, and to whom he reintroduced himself in 1878. He felt that Canon Dixon's own poetry had not had the notice it deserved and, characteristically, wrote to express, with great delicacy, his own admiration for it. Dixon, when in his turn he read some of Hopkins' work, seems to have recognised its value and importance before Bridges or, indeed, anyone else. The only other poet with whom Hopkins corresponded was Coventry Patmore, whose poetry he also admired, though Patmore, while admitting 'veins of pure gold' in Hopkins' own poems, was, as even Bridges was for some time, put off by an 'obscuring novelty of mode'.

In choosing the extracts from the letters which follow I have had to omit much that is important and revealing, but have tried to include at least some of the passages which most clearly define Hopkins' own attitude to his art.

To Robert Bridges

Stonyhurst, Whalley, Lancashire.
August 2, 1871.

My dear Bridges,

Our holidays have begun, so I will write again. I feel inclined to begin by asking whether you are secretary to the International as you seem to mean me to think nothing too bad for you but then I remember that you never relished 'the intelligent artisan'. I must tell you I am always thinking of the Communist future. The too intelligent artisan is master of the situation I believe. Perhaps it is what everyone believes, I do not see the papers or hear strangers often enough to know. It is what Carlyle has long threatened and foretold. But his writings are, as he might himself say, 'most inefficacious-strenuous heaven-protestations, caterwaul, and Cassandra-wailings'. He preaches obedience but I do not think he has done much except to ridicule instead of strengthening the hands of the powers that be. Some years ago when he published his *Shooting Niagara* he did make some practical suggestions but so vague that they should rather be called '*too* dubious moonstone-grindings and on the whole impracticable-practical unveracities'. However I am afraid some great revolution is not far off. Horrible to say, in a manner I am a Communist. Their ideal bating some things is nobler than that professed by any secular statesman I know of (I must own I live in bat-light and shoot at a venture). Besides it is just.—I do not mean the means of getting to it are. But it is a dreadful thing for the greatest and most necessary part of a very rich nation to live a hard life without dignity, knowledge, comforts, delight, or hopes in the midst of plenty—which plenty they make. They profess that they do not care what they wreck and burn, the old civilisation and order must be destroyed. This is a dreadful look out but what has the old civilisation done for them? As it at present stands in England it is itself in great measure founded on wrecking. But they got none of the spoils, they came in for nothing but harm from it then and thereafter. England has grown hugely wealthy but this wealth has not reached the working classes; I expect it has made their condition worse. Besides this iniquitous order the old civilisation embodies another order mostly old and what is new in direct entail from the old, the old religion, learning, law, art, etc and all the history that is preserved in standing monuments. But as the working classes have not been educated they know next to nothing of all this and cannot be expected to care if they destroy it. The more I look the more black and deservedly black the future looks, so I will write no more.

I can hardly believe that this is August and your letter dated May. True there has been here and I believe elsewhere no summer between. There seems some chance now. In a fortnight we are going, also for a fortnight, to Inellan in Argyleshire on the Clyde. After that I expect to pay my people a short visit down near Southampton, where they have taken a cottage. None of them are turned Catholics: I do not expect it.—

Believe me your affectionate friend

Gerard Hopkins S.J.

From a letter to Robert Bridges May 13, 1878

I enclose you my Eurydice,[1] which the *Month* refused. It is my only copy. Write no bilgewater about it: I will presently tell you what that is and till then excuse the term. I must tell you I am sorry you never read the Deutschland[2] again.

Granted that it needs study and is obscure, for indeed I was not over-desirous that the meaning of all should be quite clear, at least unmistakeable, you might, without the effort that to make it all out would seem to have required, have nevertheless read it so that lines and stanzas should be left in the memory and superficial impressions deepened, and have liked some without exhausting all. I am sure I have read and enjoyed pages of poetry that way. Why, sometimes one enjoys and admires the very lines one cannot understand, as for instance 'If it were done when 'tis done' sqq.,[3] which is all obscure and disputed, though how fine it is everybody sees and nobody disputes. And so of many more passages in Shakespere and others. Besides you would have got more weathered to the style and its features—not really odd. Now they say that vessels sailing from the port of London will take

[1] His poem 'The Loss of the Eurydice'
[2] 'The Wreck of the Deutschland'
[3] *Macbeth*, I. vii. 1

57

(perhaps it should be/ used once to take) Thames water for the voyage: it was foul and stunk at first as the ship worked but by degrees casting its filth was in a few days very pure and sweet and wholesomer and better than any water in the world. However that maybe, it is true to my purpose. When a new thing, such as my ventures in the Deutschland are, is presented us our first criticisms are not our truest, best, most homefelt, or most lasting but what come easiest on the instant. They are barbarous and like what the ignorant and the ruck say. This was so with you. The Deutschland on her first run worked very much and unsettled you, thickening and clouding your mind with vulgar mud-bottom and common sewage (I see that I am going it with the image) and just then unhappily you *drew off* your criticisms all stinking (a necessity now of the image) and bilgy, whereas if you had let your thoughts cast themselves they would have been clearer in themselves and more to my taste too. I did not heed them therefore, perceiving they were a first drawing-off. Same of the Eurydice–which being short and easy please read more than once.

From a letter to R. W. Dixon June 13, 1878

It is sad to think what disappointment must many times over have filled your heart for the darling children of your mind. Nevertheless fame whether won or lost is a thing which lies in the award of a random, reckless, incompetent, and unjust judge, the public, the multitude. The only just judge, the only just literary critic, is Christ, who prizes, is proud of, and admires, more than any man, more than the receiver himself can, the gifts of his own making. And the only real good which fame and another's praise does is to convey to us, by a channel not at all above suspicion but from circumstances in this case much less to be suspected than the channel of our own minds, some token of the judgment which a perfectly just, heedful, and wise mind, namely Christ's, passes upon our doings. Now such a token may be conveyed as well by one as by many. Therefore, believing I was able to pass a fair judgment as people go, it seemed in the circumstances a charity to tell you what I thought. For disappointment and humiliations embitter the heart and make an aching in the very bones. As far as I am concerned I say with conviction and put it on record again that you have great reason to thank God who has given you so astonishingly clear an inward eye to see what is in visible nature and in the heart such a deep insight into what is earnest, tender, and pathetic in human life and feeling as your poems display.

> Believe me, dear sir, very sincerely yours
> Gerard Hopkins S.J.

From a letter to R. W. Dixon October 5 1878

You ask, do I write verse myself. What I had written I burnt before I became a Jesuit and resolved to write no more, as not belonging to my profession, unless it were by the wish of my superiors; so for seven years I wrote nothing but two or three little presentation pieces which occasion called for. But when in the winter of '75 the Deutschland was wrecked in the mouth of the Thames and five Franciscan nuns, exiles from Germany by the Falck Laws, aboard of her were drowned I was affected by the account and happening to say so to my rector he said that he wished someone would write a poem on the subject. On this hint I set to work and, though my hand was out at first, produced one. I had long had haunting my ear the echo of a new rhythm which now I realised on paper. To speak shortly, it consists in scanning by accents or stresses alone, without any account of the number of syllables, so that a foot may be one strong syllable or it may be many light and one strong. I do not say the idea is altogether new; there are hints of it in music, in nursery rhymes and popular jingles, in the poets themselves, and, since then, I have seen it talked about as a thing possible in critics. Here are instances – '*Díng, dóng, béll*; Pússy's ín the wéll; *Whó pút* her ín? Líttle Jóhnny Thín. *Whó púlled* her óut? Líttle Jóhnny Stóut.*' For if each line has three stresses or three feet it follows that some of the feet are of one syllable only. So too '*Óne, twó*, Búckle my shóe' *passim*. In Campbell you have 'Ánd their fléet alóng the *déep próudly* shóne'–'Ít was tén of Ápril *mórn bý* the chíme' etc; in Shakspere 'Whý shd. *thís* désert bé?' corrected wrongly by the editors; in Moore a little melody I cannot quote; etc. But no one has professedly used it and made it the principle throughout, that I know of. Nevertheless to me it appears, I own, to be a better and more natural principle than the ordinary system, much more flexible, and capable of much greater effects. However I had to mark the stresses in blue chalk, and this and my rhymes carried on from one line into another and certain chimes suggested by the Welsh poetry I had been reading (what they call *cynghanedd*) and a great many more oddnesses could not but dismay an editor's eye, so that when I offered it to our magazine the *Month*, though at first they accepted it, after a time they withdrew and dared not print it. After writing this I held myself free to compose, but cannot find it in my conscience to spend time upon it; so I have done little and shall do less. But I wrote a shorter piece on the Eurydice, also in 'sprung rhythm', as I call it, but simpler, shorter, and without marks, and offered the *Month* that too, but they did not like it either. Also I have written some sonnets and a few other little things; some in sprung rhythm, with various other experiments–as 'outriding feet', that is parts of which do not count in the scanning (such as you find in Shakspere's later plays, but as a licence, whereas mine are rather calculated effects); others in the ordinary scanning *counterpointed* (this is counterpoint: '*Hóme* to his móther's hóuse *prívate* retúrned'[1] and '*Bút to vánquish* by wísdom héllish wíles'[2] etc); others, one or two, in common uncounterpointed rhythm. But even the impulse to write is wanting, for I have no thought of publishing.

I should add that Milton is the great standard in the use of counterpoint. In *Paradise Lost* and *Regained*, in the last more

[1] *Paradise Regained*, iv, 639
[2] *Ibid.*, i, 175

freely, it being an advance in his art, he employs counterpoint more or less everywhere, markedly now and then; but the choruses of *Samson Agonistes* are in my judgment counterpointed throughout; that is, each line (or nearly so) has two different coexisting scansions. But when you reach that point the secondary or 'mounted rhythm', which is necessarily a sprung rhythm, overpowers the original or conventional one and then this becomes superfluous and may be got rid of; by taking that last step you reach simple sprung rhythm. Milton must have known this but had reasons for not taking it.

From a letter to Robert Bridges February 3 1883

I quite understand what you mean about gentlemen and 'damfools'; it is a very striking thing and I could say much on the subject. I shall not say that much, but I say this: if a gentleman feels that to be what we call a gentleman is a thing essentially higher than without being a gentleman to be ever so great an artist or thinker or if, to put it another way, an artist or thinker feels that were he to become in those ways ever so great he wd. still essentially be lower than a gentleman that was no artist and no thinker—and yet to be a gentleman is but on the brim of morals and rather a thing of manners than of morals properly—then how much more must art and philosophy and manners and breeding and everything else in the world be below the least degree of true virtue. This is that chastity of mind which seems to lie at the very heart and be the parent of all other good, the seeing at once what is best, the holding to that, and the not allowing anything else whatever to be even heard pleading to the contrary. Christ's life and character are such as appeal to all the world's admiration, but there is one insight St Paul gives us of it which is very secret and seems to me more touching and constraining than everything else is:[1] This mind, he says, was in Christ Jesus—he means as man: being in the form of God—that is,

[1] Philippians ii. 5–11

finding, as in the first instant of his incarnation he did, his human nature informed by the godhead – he thought it nevertheless no snatching-matter for him to be equal with God, but annihilated himself, taking the form of servant; that is, he could not but see what he was, God, but he would see it as if he did not see it, and be it as if he were not and instead of snatching at once at what all the time was his, or was himself, he emptied or exhausted himself so far as that was possible, of godhead and behaved only as God's slave, as his creature, as man, which also he was, and then being in the guise of man humbled himself to death, the death of the cross. It is this holding of himself back, and not snatching at the truest and highest good, the good that was his right, nay his possession from a past eternity in his other nature, his own being and self, which seems to me the root of all his holiness and the imitation of this the root of all moral good in other men. I agree then, and vehemently, that a gentleman, if there is such a thing on earth, is in the position to despise the poet, were he Dante or Shakspere, and the painter, were he Angelo or Apelles, for anything in him that shewed him *not* to be a gentleman. He is in the position to do it, I say, but if he is a gentleman perhaps this is what he will not do. Which leads me to another remark.

The quality of a gentleman is so very fine a thing that it seems to me one should not be at all hasty in concluding that one possesses it. People assume that they have it, take it quite for granted, and claim the acknowledgment from others: now I should say that this also is 'no snatching-matter'. And the more a man feels what it means and is – and to feel this is certainly some part of it – the more backward he will be to think he can have realised in himself anything so perfect. It is true, there is nothing like the truth and 'the good that does itself not know scarce is'; so the perfect gentleman will know that he is the perfect gentleman. But few can be in the position to know this and, being imperfect gentlemen, it will perhaps be a point of their gentlemanliness, for a gentleman is modest, to feel that they are not perfect gentlemen.

By the by if the English race had done nothing else, yet if they left the world the notion of a gentleman, they would have done a great service to mankind.

As a fact poets and men of art are, I am sorry to say, by no means necessarily or commonly gentlemen. For gentlemen do not pander to lust or other basenesses nor, as you say, give themselves airs and affectations nor do other things to be found in modern works. And this adds a charm to everything Canon Dixon writes, that you feel he is a gentleman and thinks like one. But now I have prosed my prose and long enough.

Believe me your affectionate friend

Gerard M. Hopkins S.J.

Index of First Lines